Secrets
of the Cave
A Prehistoric Adventure

BY DEBORAH LOCK

Series Editor Deborah Lock
Project Editor Camilla Gersh
Assistant Editor Katy Lennon
Project Art Editor Hoa Luc
Editor Pomona Zaheer
Art Editor Rashika Kachroo
Producer, Pre-production Francesca Wardell
Illustrator Hoa Luc
DTP Designers Sachin Gupta, Vijay Kandwal
Picture Researcher Aditya Katyal
Managing Editor Soma B. Chowdhury
Managing Art Editor Ahlawat Gunjan

Reading Consultant Shirley Bickler
Subject Consultant Didier Bouakaze-Khan

First published in Great Britain by
Dorling Kindersley Limited
80 Strand, London, WC2R 0RL

Copyright © 2015 Dorling Kindersley Limited
A Penguin Random House Company
10 9 8 7 6 5 4 3 2 1
001–271019–Apr/2015

Published in Great Britain by Dorling Kindersley Limited.

A CIP catalogue record for this book
is available from the British Library.
ISBN: 978-0-2411-8277-2

Printed and bound in China

The publisher would like to thank the following for their kind permission to reproduce their photographs:
(Key: a-above; b-below/bottom; c-center; f-far; l-left; r-right; t-top)
1 Alamy Images: Glasshouse Images. **5 Corbis**: Bettmann. **8 Alamy Images**: Heritage Image Partnership Ltd (bc);
Dorling Kindersley: The Natural History Museum, London (cra); **The Pitt Rivers Museum**, University of Oxford (cr).
9 Alamy Images: John Angerson (crb); **Dorling Kindersley**: The Art Gallery Collection (cra). **Dorling Kindersley**: The Natural History
Museum, London (tr). **11 Getty Images**: Gamma-Rapho Via Getty Images/Pierre Briolle. **12–13 Getty Images**: Alinari
via Getty Images. **16–17 Alamy Images**: Ray Roberts. **19 Getty Images**: AFP/Lionel Bonaventure. **22 Dorling Kindersley**:
James Jordan (bl, r). **23 Dorling Kindersley**: James Jordan (l, r). **25 Dorling Kindersley**: Geoff Brightling/ESPL-modelmaker.
26 Dorling Kindersley: The Natural History Museum, London (clb); **Photo Scala, Florence**: DeAgostini Picture Library/Scala,
Florence (br). **27 Dorling Kindersley**: The Natural History Museum, London (tl); The Pitt Rivers Museum, University of Oxford
(cl); The Museum of London (tr). **31–32 Getty Images**: Alinari via Getty Images. **32–33 Getty Images**: The LIFE Picture
Collection/Ralph Morse. **35 Getty Images**: AFP/Pierre Andrieu. **38–39 Getty
Images**: DEA/G. Dagli Orti/De Agostini. **40 Dreamstime.com**: Somartin (cb). **40–41 Dreamstime.com**: Dmitrii Kiselev (b).
42 Dreamstime.com: Aleksandr Evseev (tl). **50–51 Getty Images**: Gamma-Rapho Via Getty Images/Serge De Sazo.
52–53 Getty Images: AFP/Philippe Wojazer. **55 Getty Images**: Time & Life Pictures/Ralph Morse. **56 Science Photo Library**:
University Of Manchester/Michael Donne (cla, br). **57 Science Photo Library**: University Of Manchester/Michael Donne.
59 Alamy Images: Hemis (cb); Wild Places/Chris Howes (t). **62 Corbis**: The Gallery Collection. **67 Corbis**: The Gallery
Collection. **70 Dreamstime.com**: Robin Kizzar (cr). **71 Dorling Kindersley**: The Science Museum, London (cra); **Dreamstime.com**:
William Berry (cr). **Fotolia**: Jose Manuel Gelpi (bc); Mari art (bl). **73 Getty Images**: DEA/A. Dagli Orti/De Agostini. **75 Alamy
Images**: Robert Harding Picture Library Ltd. **77 Corbis**: Hemis/Jean-Daniel Sudres. **79 Getty Images**: AFP. **80-81 Getty Images**:
AFP/Lionel Bonaventure. **88 Dorling Kindersley**: The Museum of London (ca, cra). **99 Corbis**: Reuters/Philippe Wojazer.
100 Corbis. **102–103 Corbis**: Reuters/Philippe Wojazer. **104 Dorling Kindersley**: Simon Jackson Carter (cl). **105 Alamy Images**:
The Print Collector (tl). **Dorling Kindersley**: The Royal British Columbia Museum, Victoria, Canada (cl). **107 PENGUIN and the
Penguin logo are trademarks of Penguin Books Ltd: Stig Of The Dump by Clive king © Puffin. 113 Getty Images**: Gamma-Rapho
Via Getty Images/Serge De Sazo. **114 Getty Images**: Time & Life Pictures/Ralph Morse. **115 Getty Images**: Gamma-Rapho
via Getty Images/Jerome Chatin. **116 Corbis**: JAI/Amar Grover (cl). **116–117 Dreamstime.com**: Sommersby (antique photo
frame reproduced four times). **117 Corbis**: Frederic Soltan (cr); Robert Harding World Imagery/Gavin Hellier (tl). **Getty Images**:
Seth Joel (bl). **118 Dorling Kindersley**: The Natural History Museum, London (cla). **Jacket images: Front: Corbis**: Reuters/
Philippe Wojazer; **Dorling Kindersley**: The Museum of London (clb/spear); **Photo Scala, Florence**: DeAgostini Picture Library/
Scala, Florence (clb/burin); **Back: Getty Images**: Alinari Archives (t); **Spine: Getty Images**: AFP/Jeff Pachoud (b). **Endpapers:**
Dorling Kindersley: The Royal British Columbia Museum, Victoria, Canada

All other images © Dorling Kindersley
For further information see: www.dkimages.com

A WORLD OF IDEAS:
SEE ALL THERE IS TO KNOW

Contents

DISCLAIMER

This narrative has been inspired by the cave paintings of Lascaux and others in the south of France during the Upper Palaeolithic Age.

Because of the lack of written evidence, we can only guess how prehistoric people might have lived. The story of Jason is based on a range of theories about the way people lived in prehistoric times. The facts may have been different.

The activities undertaken in this book were done by actual Palaeolithic people. Please check with an adult before attempting.

No animals were harmed during the making of this book.

Jason's journey is only a story, but the rest might be true!

Don't believe everything you read!

LOCATION

The year is 17,000BCE. Since humans evolved in Africa six million years ago, they have spread across Europe as far as Britain, Germany and Russia, and into Asia. In southern Europe, groups of people are beginning to make and use a range of tools. It is here that our story is set.

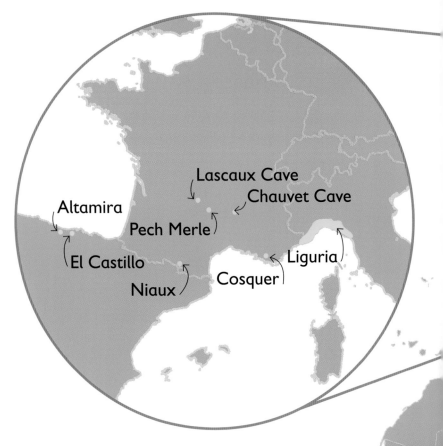

FRANCE

SPAIN

ITALY

Prehistoric Time Chart

PALAEOLITHIC 2.6 MYA (MILLION YEARS AGO)—10,000 YEARS AGO

LOWER PALAEOLITHIC
2.6 MYA—300,000 years ago

2.6 million years ago
Homo habilis, the first of the *Homo* genus, appears; he chips flakes off pebbles to form rough tools for chopping, scraping or cutting.

MIDDLE PALAEOLITHIC
300,000—30,000 years ago

200,000 years ago
Homo sapiens, the first modern human, appears; he uses the 'prepared-core technique' for the first time. In this method, a core is carefully chipped on one side to produce a flake of a certain size and shape with one blow.

UPPER PALAEOLITHIC
50,000—10,000 years ago

33,000–29,000 years ago
Aurignacian period: people begin to use a wide variety of flint and bone tools, including the burin (see pp26–27) for carving, to make the earliest-known cave art and figurative art.

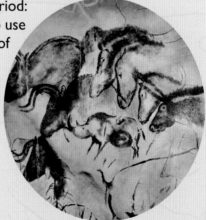

PALAEOLITHIC
UPPER PALAEOLITHIC
50,000–10,000 years ago

27,000–19,000 years ago
Gravettian period:
people hunt large animals in groups
and create bone and shell jewellery
and figurines called 'Venuses'.

21,000–18,000 years ago
Solutrean period:
people create finely carved blades
and arrowheads in the shape of
laurel leaves and use bone needles
to sew clothes.

17,000–11,500 years ago
Magdalenian period:
people use elaborate tools made of carved
bone and antler and reach a high standard
of cave painting in sites such as Lascaux.

MESOLITHIC
10,000–7,000
YEARS AGO

10,000–7,000 years ago
People begin to use tiny carved
tools called microliths.

NEOLITHIC
7,000–5,000
YEARS AGO

c.7,000 years ago
People begin farming and
are able to create permanent
settlements. They use small
cutting tools such as adzes.

CHAPTER ONE
The Chinese Horse

The ground shook as the herd of horses broke into a stampede in panic. Their thundering hooves kicked up the mud as they galloped across the grass-covered valley. Clouds of snorted breath puffed from their nostrils in the cold, early-spring air. Droplets of damp sweat trickled through their thick, shaggy manes and down their flanks.

The hunters, who had crept up behind to surprise and startle the herd, were now running beside them. Like a pack of hungry wolves, they eyed the herd, figuring out which ones they would aim for. They screamed and yelled to further confuse the horses.

Moments before, the herd had been quietly grazing until they spotted the hunters close by in the longer grass. Now the terrified creatures were racing towards the narrow end of the valley to escape. They were unaware that greater danger lurked hidden in the long grass ahead.

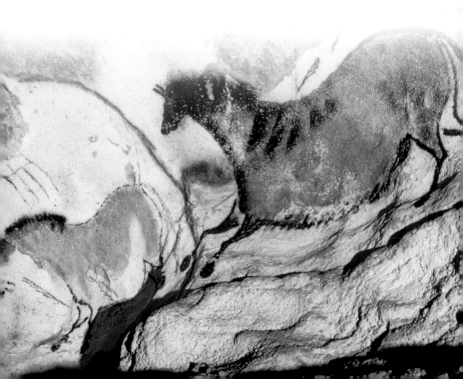

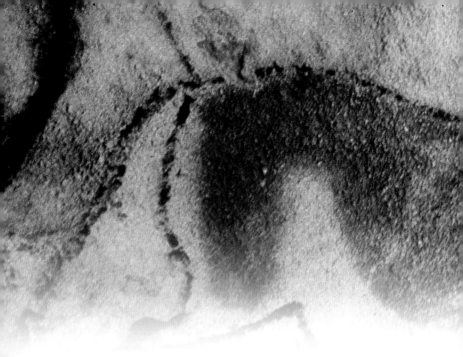

A handful of men draped in warm horse skins was crouched low, spears at the ready in hands by their sides. They watched and waited, eagerly anticipating the fast-approaching moment to launch an ambush.

As the stampede drew closer and closer, the hunters leapt up and threw their spears. The long wooden rods tipped with deadly, jagged flint-heads whizzed with a swift whistle of wind slicing through the air.

12

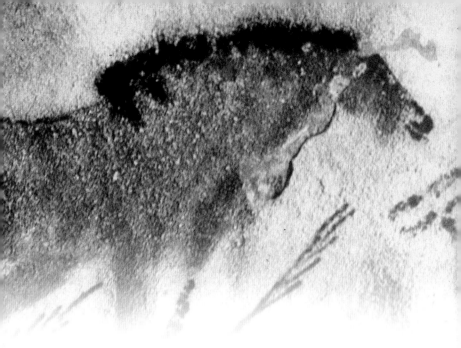

Each arrowhead found its target, and the injured beasts collapsed onto the ground. Other horses stumbled in the confusion, while still others leapt over the fallen bodies. The horses slipped on the waterlogged ground, which had been soaked by the recent rains.

At the point where the valley narrowed, the running hunters forced the flustered horses to squeeze together.

Taking advantage of this position, they jabbed their bone-barbed harpoons into the passing horses. The bone hooks tore at the horses' flesh.

The last of the horses pounded through the narrow gap into the next valley. The hunters whooped and jeered after them. Then silence fell. Eight injured horses lay scattered across the ground. Horse meat would make a pleasant change from the reindeer meat the clan had eaten all winter.

Watching the action from a nearby hillside was a young boy, about 12 years old. With keen eyes, he had observed the skill and the tactics of the hunters. His father Ja was one of the best, and he was easy to spot as he was taller and stronger than the other hunters. The boy looked down at the blade flake that he had been preparing in the palm of his left hand. "Will I ever be as brave as my father?" he wondered. As the son of Ja, named Jason, the rest of the clan expected him to become a great hunter as well. He only had a year left to train before he took on the great challenge for his initiation from boyhood into adulthood.

Jason slammed the antler hammer down into an upright flint, which was positioned above a piece of rock. The force of the hammer's blow punched the upright flint into the rock, creating a shock wave. A long, delicate blade flake broke away. Jason picked it up to check its side-on shape. Disappointed, he threw it among his discarded pile. None of these had the triangular or trapezium side-on shape that was expected. "Will I ever be good enough?" he worried. "Will I be ready in time? How will Father react if I fail?"

Jason's hammering quickened as his mind raced with worries, but also with excitement. This summer he would be joining the hunters in action.

"Jason!" The echo from his name being shouted across the valley disturbed his wandering thoughts. Looking up, he saw his father waving his arms, summoning his son over. The hunters had finished tying leather straps around the dead horses' feet and threading wooden poles between the

front and the back. The horses were ready to be lifted and taken back to the cave. This task would require a team effort.

Jason quickly gathered up his blade flakes and antler tools, tucking them into a leather pouch, and raced down the hillside. His father did not like to be kept waiting.

"Pick up spears," instructed Ja abruptly when Jason reached him.

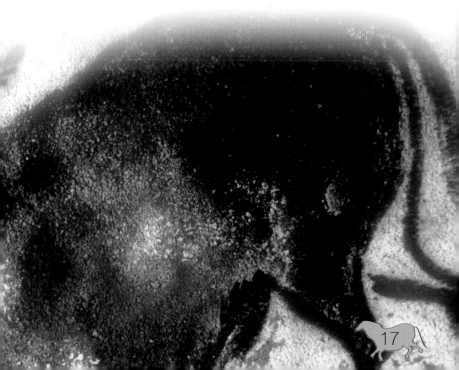

Without hesitation, Jason went over
to the pile of blood-spattered wooden
spears and bone-barbed harpoons
that the hunters had used. Picking
them up, he carefully balanced them
across his arms. He then followed
the hunters, who carried the poles
with the prizes of the hunt, through the
narrow gap and into the next valley.

In a victorious procession, the
hunting party followed a well-worn
path up towards an opening in the
rock face above them. Over the top of
his burden, Jason glanced down to the
valley below. The shaggy horses had
returned to graze on the fresh new
shoots of grass. Aurochs (wild cattle)
had joined them, returning from
their winter feeding grounds
in the warmer sites south of here.
The reindeer also contentedly nibbled
on new leaves just unfolding from
the buds on the trees.

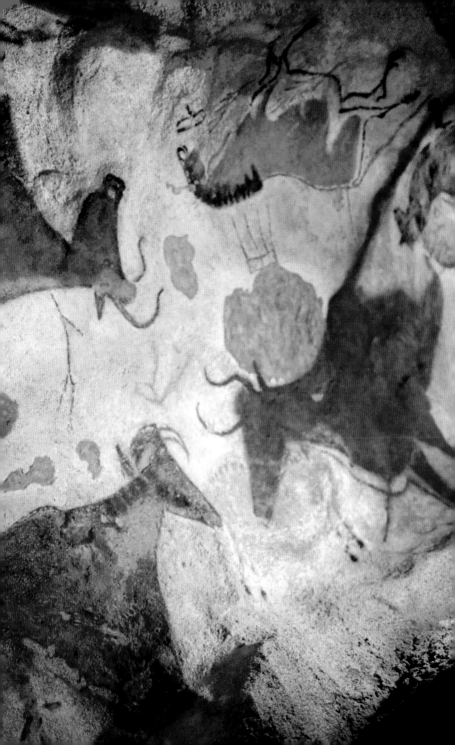

Jason smiled, taking in the fresh springtime air.

"Jason!" shouted his father. Jason could tell from the angry tone that his father was annoyed with his dawdling.

"Sorry," Jason called back, sheepishly.

"Caw! Caw!" cackled a crow sitting in the branches of a tree above his head. Jason looked up and shivered at the sight of the large black bird.

"Not a good sign," he thought, hurrying as much as he could to catch up.

An immense crackling fire was already burning brightly when the hunters arrived back at the cave. The smell of crushed herbs, gathered that day by the women, lingered in the air. Spirits were joyful. There would be a feast tonight.

> Why did Jason 'shiver' when he saw the crow?

Unusual Suspects

About two million years ago in Africa, the *Homo* genus evolved from ape-like ancestors. If any of these early suspects lined up here look familiar, it is because we are closely related to them all.

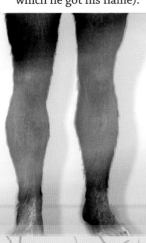

Homo erectus
1.8 MYA–300,000 years ago
H. erectus had a large face, powerful build and upright stance (from which he got his name).

Homo habilis
1.9–1.6 MYA (million years ago)
H. habilis had a big brain and was smart enough to make tools.

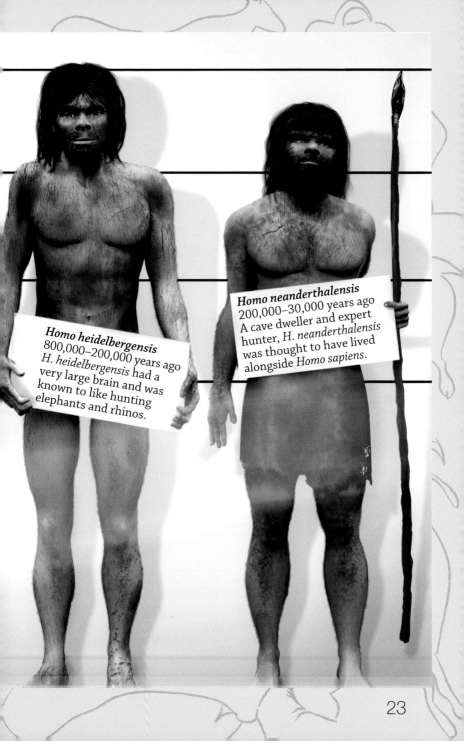

Homo heidelbergensis
800,000–200,000 years ago
H. heidelbergensis had a very large brain and was known to like hunting elephants and rhinos.

Homo neanderthalensis
200,000–30,000 years ago
A cave dweller and expert hunter, H. neanderthalensis was thought to have lived alongside Homo sapiens.

23

Introducing... *Homo sapiens*

Early *Homo sapiens* possessed several important physical features that gave them unique abilities, such as walking upright and sophisticated thinking. These provided a distinct evolutionary advantage over other species.

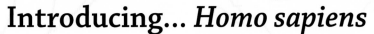

large skull to accommodate big brain

short, narrow pelvis supports upper body and enables the body to tilt, maintaining balance when walking

flexible hands and thumbs allow precision grip

well-developed arches and wide heels allow the foot to push off with toes and absorb the forces of walking

large big toes aligned with other toes allow the foot to push off

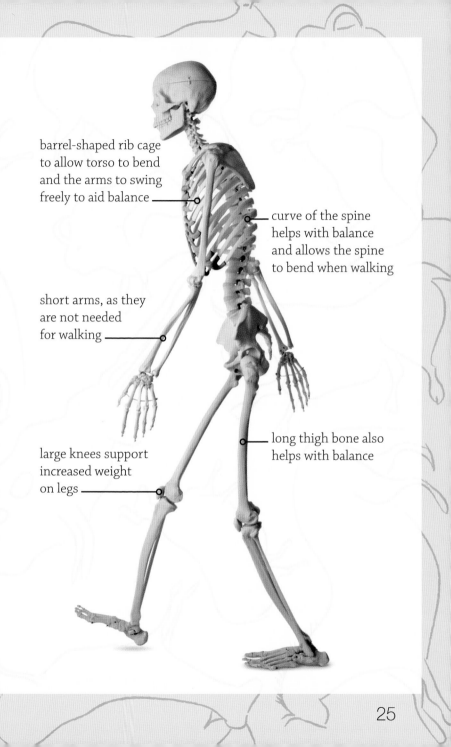

barrel-shaped rib cage
to allow torso to bend
and the arms to swing
freely to aid balance

curve of the spine
helps with balance
and allows the spine
to bend when walking

short arms, as they
are not needed
for walking

long thigh bone also
helps with balance

large knees support
increased weight
on legs

Tool Time!

Before the discovery of metal, *Homo sapiens* had to make tools using stone and bone. They learned that certain tools would make hunting animals and gathering food easier. Here are some of the tools that *Homo sapiens* from the Magdalenian period would have used.

CORE-AND-HAMMER SET

What every prehistoric hunter needs to ensure that he gets the best and sharpest stone flakes for his hand-axe, arrows and spear!

- Core is obsidian stone to create strong and sharp flakes
- Antler hammer is sturdy and durable, with a long handle that fits comfortably in the hand
- Stone flakes are multi-purpose objects that can be used as hand-axes or arrow tips
- Essential part of every hunter's toolkit
- Set comes with a handy leather travel pouch

Antler hammer

Flint flake

Prepared rock core

BURIN

BONE HARPOON

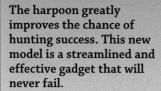

The harpoon greatly improves the chance of hunting success. This new model is a streamlined and effective gadget that will never fail.

- Angle of teeth has been carefully calculated to ensure maximum resistance – once the harpoon has met its target, it cannot be removed easily

- Lightweight harpoon can easily be attached to spears for accurate aim when targeting an animal from a distance

- Can be used multiple times and is a must-have for every hunter

SCRAPER

Don't be caught short without the new Stone Scraper 5000! This innovative device will make animal-skinning quick and easy so that you can have your dinner cooking or your fur blanket ready in no time!

- Flat side glides effortlessly between the hide and meat of your chosen animal, with only minimal pressure required

- Perfect for cleaning animal hides

- Razor-sharp edge will leave the skin smooth and ready to use

The perfect precision tool for the prehistoric artist, this utensil is essential for creating intricate carvings on wood, or bone weapons and instruments.

- Razor-sharp point is excellent for carving delicate pictures but is also strong enough to chip away large chunks of wood or bone

- New lightweight model is slim and comfortable to hold

HUNTER-GATHERER
Four Seasons Restaurant

At the Hunter-Gatherer Restaurant, we pride ourselves on offering the finest seasonal fare. We aim to give customers an authentic 'back-to-nature' experience.

SPRING

Starter
Sautéed mice

Main course
Minted horse steak with root vegetable purée

Dessert
Fresh strawberries (v)

SUMMER

Starter
Dried fish slices

Main course
Salmon parcels with a peppery watercress salad

Dessert
Squashed blackberries (v)

All produce is organic and responsibly sourced from the land around the Dordogne River.

AUTUMN

Starter
Root vegetable soup (v)

Main course
Bison and truffle hotpot

Dessert
Apple and walnut
salad (v)

WINTER

Starter
Duck satay skewers

Main course
Spit-roasted reindeer

Dessert
Walnuts with berries (v)

WEEKDAY SPECIALS
Beetle-larva canapés
Mammoth stew
Nuts with honey

DRINKS

Mineral water
Crushed berries
Ox blood

RESERVATIONS
To make a reservation,
please e-mail us at
reservations@hunter.gatherer.com

(v) suitable for vegetarians

CHAPTER TWO
The Hall of Bulls

A silence fell over the gathered clans, as a faint glow broke through the darkness. A hundred faces watched the dawn's summer sunlight peep above the dark horizon. The first rays touched the cave's entrance. Then the opening became clearer and brighter in the swiftly growing daylight.

Emerging from the cave, a half-man, half-unicorn figure appeared and stood in the doorway.

The single-horned headdress
completely covered the man's face.
Adorned in a silvery cloak made
of animal skin, the shaman glowed
in the sunlight. Jason watched
open-mouthed in awe. This was his
favourite celebration of the year, when
the shaman summoned the spirits,
weaving magic for successful hunting.
   The shaman raised his arms and
pawed the air. Then he turned to lead
the way into the cave of Lascaux.
Respectfully, the clans followed.

Staying close to his family, Jason descended the 30 steps. Ja held a spoon-shaped sandstone lamp. It glowed brightly, and its burning wick smelt of juniper. The flickering light guided their footsteps through the network of passages. Out of the shadows, eyes on animal heads painted on the walls flashed.

Jason gasped as the corridor opened up into a great cavern. The horn-shaped, firelit torches revealed the gallery of proud stags, running horses and countless bulls.

When each clan entered, it moved to its familiar, assigned position in the

hall-like room. Jason's clan always sat beneath the dark-maned horse and the half-drawn starlit bull. Jason gazed up towards the majestic and powerful beasts towering above his head. His heartbeat quickened. These were not the animals that they hunted daily for food. These held the power of magic.

Everyone sat on the chalky floor. There was not much room, especially for taller people such as Ja. Jason was squashed against him.

The shaman stood still in the centre of the cavern. All eyes were on him, watching and waiting.

A low hum began. The people joined in, as a mysterious wafting of a deep note increased in strength like a wave. The shaman pawed the ground with his feet. The people picked up the beat with their stamping feet. Bodies rocked and swayed. The hall filled with vibrations as the sounds bounced off the walls.

Like a lively unicorn, the shaman's movements quickened. His head nodded, his arms pawed, and his body moved in a trance-like dance. His hum became cries as he summoned the spirits to enter his body. Jason's hum resonated in his head. He wondered if the cave would burst open.

As the hum grew in a crescendo into a pulsing heartbeat, the shaman picked up a hollowed-out bone and climbed a wooden scaffold. Positioning the bone close to the ceiling, he gently blew through it. A cloud of black,

powdered-manganese pigment
sprayed out. Blow after blow,
the features of a bull's face gradually
took shape on the wall.
   "Which bull would this be?"
wondered Jason. The bull with four
stars that can be seen in a winter's sky
already proudly adorned the wall.

Still in his trance, the shaman mixed some red, iron-oxide clay with some cave water and rubbed this pigment with his hands over the bull's body. This gave the body a radiating glow. The natural curve of the wall suggested the bull had a full belly.

Jason began to feel uncomfortable. By now, they had all been sitting for some time. Jason wished he could wriggle, but he was worried about disturbing Ja next to him. Everyone was still absorbed in the humming. "Maybe no one will notice a little wriggle," Jason thought. Suddenly, the sharp pain of a cramp zapped up Jason's leg.

"Aagh!" he gasped, jerking his leg to grab the aching muscle.

Ja turned and scowled. "Sit still," he hissed with annoyance.

Jason tried to bear the pain, rubbing the muscle until the ache had gone.

The
shaman
dipped his
fingers into
a paste
of black
manganese,
and, with long
strokes, he created
the spiralled horns.
This was to
be another
majestic bull.
He carefully
filled in the
face and horns
with white clay
made of calcite.
Unexpectedly, the
shaman stopped
painting; his
body shook
violently.

Jason was taken aback by the weird movement, which looked like an owl trying to stop itself from falling off a branch. He wanted to laugh, and his body began to shake. He caught the eye of Ja glaring at him. "Oh no," Jason thought. "I'm in trouble again!"

With arms raised, the shaman let out a piercing cry, summoning the spirits of the earth, sky and water. The hum gathered pace and became louder and louder. The pounding of feet shook the ground. The shaman once again picked up the bone and blew seven marks around the bull's eyes. Jason recognised them as the tight cluster of stars seen sparkling on clear nights.

The shaman turned to face the clans. Their hum became frenzied. Some people screamed out; others began to sway, forcing the whole crowd to rock. Jason felt the warmth from the fire's heat tingle his skin, and he caught a whiff of the fire's choking smoke and the smell of Ja's sweaty body pressing up against him. Overwhelmed by the atmosphere, his head became fuzzy and faint, and he blacked out.

When Jason opened his eyes, he was only aware of Ja shaking him violently. The cavern was silent and empty. The bull's face glared down at him in the flickering torchlight.

THE BEST OF

THE
HOMO SAPIENS

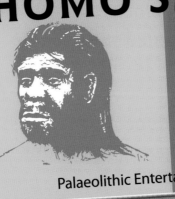

Palaeolithic Entertainment presents

I ❤ HS

40

The Homo Sapiens are world renowned for their spiritual performances, which have been described by many as 'out of this world'. The voice was the first musical instrument used by the Homo Sapiens. Their unique sound makes use of feet-stamping, clapping and haunting ritual chanting. All instruments played in the band are handmade with natural materials, sourced from bones and tree trunks.

THE MUSICIANS

Max Homo Sapien, lead singer. He began singing as soon as he learned to talk. He is skilled at humming and at imitating animal sounds.

Leo Homo Sapien on bone whistle. Leo's whistle was made by boring holes into hollow animal bone to make a flute.

Sue Homo Sapien, hand-clapper. Clapping is used to create rhythm in songs and chants.

Dan Homo Sapien on the horn. Dan blows through his animal horn to make a trumpet sound.

Jen Homo Sapien on the drums. Animal skin has been stretched over hollow tree trunks or wooden frames so that Jen can hit it with hands or sticks to help keep rhythm.

THE BEST OF THE HOMO SAPIENS

Catching Up with Shaman Ray

Hi, I'm Peter Stein, and welcome to *Catching Up*, the show that brings you up close with Lascaux's most illustrious citizens. Today I'm meeting Shaman Ray and hearing about his out-of-this-world experiences. Welcome, Shaman Ray.

So, what exactly does a shaman do?

Thank you, Peter. I organise and manage ceremonies and lead rituals for the clans. I can also cure illnesses and provide counselling using my special powers. I am greatly respected and powerful and receive gifts from the people in return.

How did you become a shaman?

I received my special powers in an inspirational moment. Some shamans are born with their powers, while others gain them through training. We are all specially chosen by the spirits, though.

What special powers do you have?

Through a state of trance, I enter the animal spirit world, and the spirits transfer their powers to me. With these powers, I can tell the future, diagnose and cure illnesses and cast magical spells for successful hunting. Other skills include singing, dancing, magic tricks and ventriloquism (throwing my voice).

Which animal spirits have helped you?

My spirit is the stag, but this is sometimes combined with the bison's spirit. Other shamans become fish, bird, unicorn or rhinoceros spirits. There are also some who transform into a combination of ibex and horse, or bison and boar spirits.

What's it like to be in a trance?

I can't remember. The spirit takes over, and I am not myself, so I have no recollection of the event after it.

Star Map

The bull painted by the shaman in the cave and the marks around the bull's eyes represent the star constellation Taurus and the Pleiades star cluster. These can be seen in the sky in the winter in the Northern Hemisphere. Take a look at this star map for February and see if you can find Taurus and the Pleiades in the sky at night, just as the people of Lascaux did!

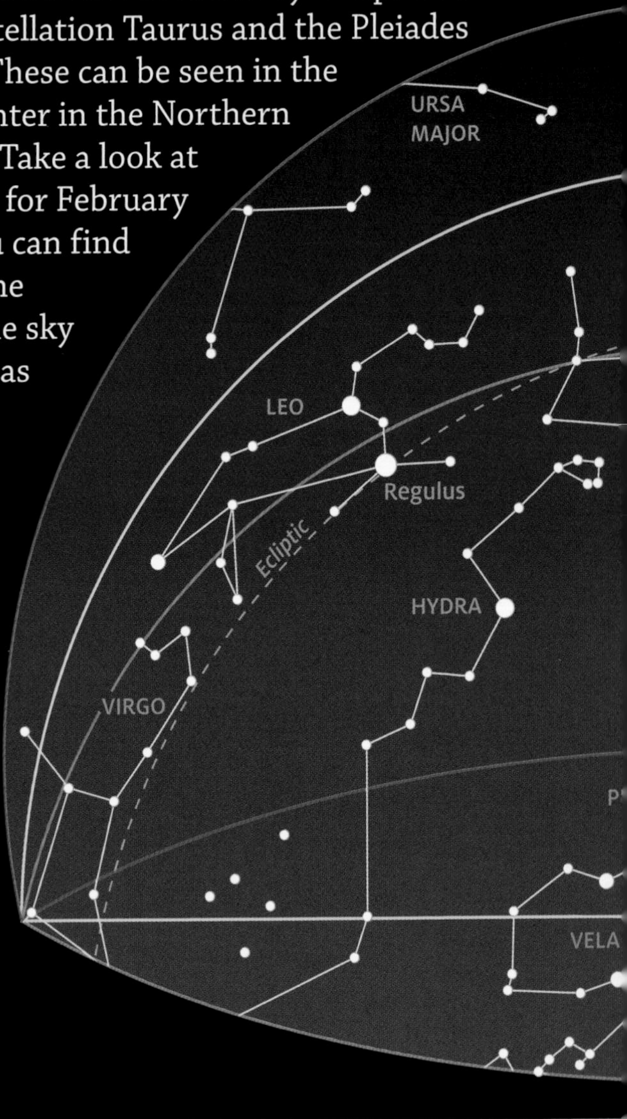

URSA MAJOR

LEO

Regulus

Ecliptic

HYDRA

VIRGO

P

VELA

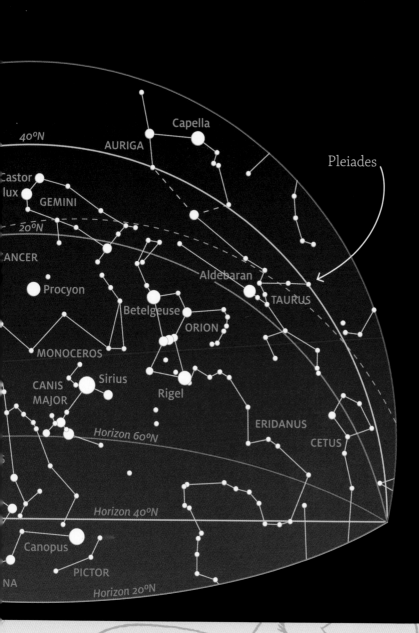

Pleiades

40°N

AURIGA

Capella

Castor
lux

GEMINI

20°N

CANCER

Procyon

Aldebaran

TAURUS

Betelgeuse

ORION

MONOCEROS

CANIS
MAJOR

Sirius

Rigel

ERIDANUS

CETUS

Horizon 60°N

Horizon 40°N

Canopus

PICTOR

NA

Horizon 20°N

CHAPTER THREE
The Crossed Bison

"Mammoth!" whispered Ja, as he beckoned to the other hunters to surround the beast. Stealthily, Jason moved with the hunters through the trees. Carefully, he placed his feet so as not to disturb a twig on the forest floor, and in turn alert the grazing mammoth to their presence. The woolly mammoth continued to rub its long, curved tusks against the bark of a tree to loosen strips. Its trunk then broke off the strips and curled up, putting them into its mouth to gnaw them with its teeth.

Suddenly, a crow cawed above Jason's head, alerting the mammoth. Disturbed from its meal, the creature whisked around as the hunters emerged from the shadows, spears ready to throw. The mammoth roared and swung its tusks from side to side, threatening and daring them to come closer. The crow flapped into the air. Startled, the mammoth charged in the direction it had come from – straight towards Jason.

Jason's pulse raced. "No!" he screamed. Terrified, he stood rooted to the spot. Fear gripped him, and sweat poured down his face. The mammoth's eyes were glaring with anger and gazed directly at Jason as it charged.

"This is it," thought Jason. "I've failed!"

Jason jerked awake from his nightmare. The cave was dark except for the glowing embers of the fire. Around him, the bodies of his clan lay sleeping peacefully. The rain poured down outside. His body was damp with sweat, and his heart was racing. Relieved that the mammoth hunt was only in his imagination, he pulled the bearskin rug back over and curled up once more to sleep.

"Jason!" shouted Ja, shaking him awake. "You lazy boy, get up now!"

As Jason opened his eyes, he realised the cave was now lit with early-morning autumn sunlight. Around him, women were busy shaking the bear rugs and gathering them up. Other women were clearing up the fish and fruit from the meal area. The hunters were all ready with weapons in their hands, eager to get started.

Towering over Jason, Ja threw his horse-skin tunic at him to put on.

"Time to go!" Ja turned away in disgust, paced over to the waiting hunters and led them out of the cave.

Hurriedly, Jason dressed, slipped on his leather moccasins, grabbed his spear and ran after them. At the entrance to the cave, his younger sister rushed over to hand him some blackberries and two apples to eat on his way.

"Thanks, Jasmine," Jason said to her gratefully.

Jason tried to hurry to catch up with the hunting party, but the pathway leading back down to the valley was very slippery. The water started to soak into the leather of his shoes. Over the past week, the autumn rains had poured down. On some days, the torrents had been too bad for the hunters and gatherers even to go out. Everyone had become restless cooped up in the cave. Jason had not minded though. He had been glad for the break from his hunting training over the past five months. Ja was a strict teacher and had taken him out for

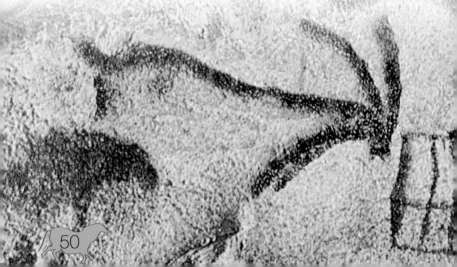

further practice even after a full day of hunting with the group. When the others had gone home, Jason was kept behind to strengthen his spear-throwing and to build up his stamina with extra running. Ja always expected more from him.

As Jason looked down to the valley, he saw the river, full of water, flowing swiftly. The parched grass of the hot summer had now been revived to a rich green. The vast bison herds had migrated to the valley, and ibexes, cattle and horses grazed among them.

Jason finally caught up with
the hunting party at the bottom
of the path. They were all crouched,
watching the bison herd graze.
Just killing one of the male
bison would feed
the clan for ten days.
This would not be
easy though,
because each
bison was taller
and more than
ten times
heavier than
a man. The
hunters' spear–
throws would need to
be accurate and powerful
to get through a bison's shaggy
mane and thick fur. Each bison
had short horns, which could easily
maim and kill a hunter if it charged.

A team effort was needed if
the hunters had any chance of
making a successful kill.
 Ja waved his arm to beckon the
running party to move
downwind of the herd.
Jason was among
this small group
who would
startle the herd
and separate
the chosen
bison. They
began to creep
stealthily through
the grass, like
a pack of lionesses
approaching a water
buffalo. Meanwhile, Ja and
the ambush party moved to the spot
where the bison would be led and
the kill would take place.

Moving closer and closer, Jason approached. He could hear the bisons' snorts and the grass being ripped up and chewed in their mouths. Just a bit further now.

Suddenly, Jason slipped on a pile of dung. In surprise, he let out a startled cry as his foot gave way, and he toppled over.

"Arrgh!"

The bison nearest to him looked up, eyes glaring straight in Jason's direction. In a split second, the whole herd was on the move. The alarm of the hunters' presence had been given, and the stampede began.

It was too soon for the running party. They leapt from their crawling positions, but they had not been close enough to the targeted bison. They ran following the herd hopelessly, but they had no chance now to separate any of them. The hunt had failed.

The bison resettled to graze in a safer position at the far end of the valley, out of reach of the hunters. Ja stormed ahead of the disappointed ambush party, ambling back to regroup.

Jason stood dejected, waiting for the barrage of insults from his father that would certainly follow. Scowling and seething, Ja approached him.

"Jason, home!" fumed Ja, barely able to control his anger.

Sullenly, Jason slunk away. The hunting party would try again, perhaps to catch an ox, but he no longer had a part to play.

Facial Reconstruction

When scientists find an ancient skull, they can do a facial reconstruction that enables them to see what the owner of the skull looked like. Here is how they do it.

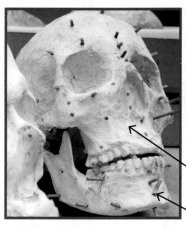

1 Pegs are inserted over a cast of the skull. These show the depth of facial flesh on a person of the same sex and age.

cast of well-preserved skull

pegs inserted by modeller

2 Clay is built around the temples and jaw, representing the muscles and underlying flesh.

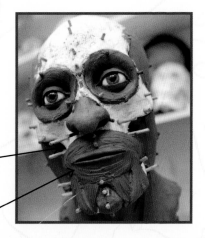

clay built up on skull

face starts to take shape

3 When the pegs are completely covered, the clay (representing the skin) is smoothed over the whole skull.

clay added to full depth

shape of nose is guessed at

facial features guessed at

4 The biggest guesses must be made in the final stages, when the hair and other features are added.

VISIT THE WORLD-FAMOUS LASCAUX CAVES

The Grotte de Lascaux World Heritage Site in France is actually several caves containing marvellously preserved paintings that were made by people 17,000 years ago. They show bison, stags, horses and bulls. They are among the finest examples of prehistoric art in existence.

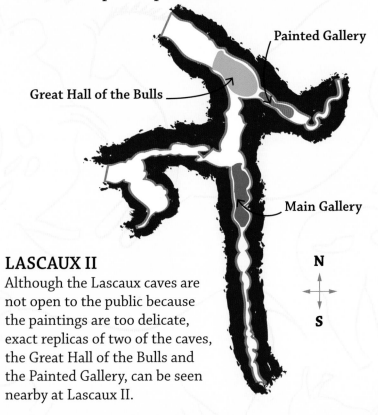

Painted Gallery

Great Hall of the Bulls

Main Gallery

N
S

LASCAUX II

Although the Lascaux caves are not open to the public because the paintings are too delicate, exact replicas of two of the caves, the Great Hall of the Bulls and the Painted Gallery, can be seen nearby at Lascaux II.

LE THOT

A visit to this prehistoric 'theme park' will complement your trip to the cave, with dioramas of prehistoric scenes, live animals like those depicted in the paintings and a film explaining how Lascaux II was made. It's fun for the whole family!

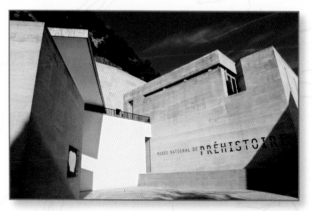

NATIONAL MUSEUM OF PREHISTORY

A small diversion will bring you to this museum in the tiny, picturesque village of Les Eyzies-de-Tayac. It contains all the most important artefacts found in the Lascaux caves and elsewhere in France. It is not to be missed!

CHAPTER FOUR
The Rhinoceros

Jasmine reached her fingers out to pick the biggest blackberry on the bush. It was the perfect ripeness, and she knew it would be juicy and sweet to eat. She was tempted to pop it into her mouth rather than into the leather basket she was carrying, but she resisted. She knew how important it was to gather every single fruit and nut to help the clan through the winter ahead.

The forest was radiant in autumnal colours. Reds, oranges and yellows glowed among the various shades of brown of the dying leaves. All around Jasmine, the women and other girls were busily gathering anything edible they could find. Some broke off roots using sharp edges of flint, and others scraped away the soil with tips of bones to find tubers. These were foods they could store through the winter.

Tara, Jasmine's mother, signalled to the women that it was time to return. They needed to get back to the cave and prepare the fire before the men returned from their hunt.

The women picked up their heavily laden baskets and happily chatted as they wandered back through the forest. The women emerged into the wide expanse of the valley. Jasmine spied the herd of reindeer and knew that somewhere in the grass near them, Jason would be crouched, waiting for the moment to start running.

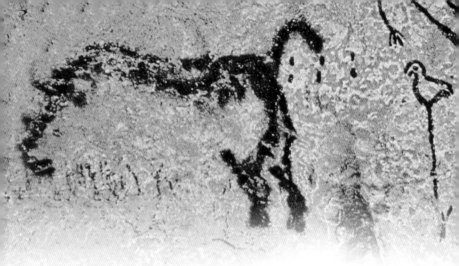

Suddenly, a bellowing sound nearby broke the silence. The women stood still. About 50 metres ahead, a single woolly rhinoceros was glaring straight at the group. Jasmine shivered in fright. The beast was snorting. It was a confused young male that had been left behind. The herd of woolly rhinos had left on their winter migration to warmer areas a few days ago.

Tara signalled to the women to move slowly as a group further along the forest's edge and then take a wide arc around the rhino.

From his crouching position, Jason had also heard the bellow. He turned and saw the danger the women were in. "Should I alert Father?" he wondered. "That would mean giving my position away to the reindeer, messing up the hunt again." No longer watching the deer, Jason watched as the women edged their way around the rhino.

The rhino continued to glare at the women, nodding its head in a threatening display.

Without warning, one of the young girls broke away from the group in panic and started running ahead. Jason gasped as he recognised that the girl was Jasmine.

The rhino had spotted her, and it scraped the ground with its hooves. With a bellow that echoed around the valley, the rhino broke into a run.

Without a moment's hesitation, Jason leapt up and began hollering and wildly waving his arms. Shocked by the sudden noise, the rhino changed direction and began running full charge straight at Jason.

In that split second, the peaceful valley turned into a scene of mayhem. Now alerted, the other hunters joined in the hollering as they ran towards the thundering rhino to support Jason. Tara and the other women were able to catch up with Jasmine and form a protective group around her. They watched in horror as the hunters threw their spears at the rhino. Some spears wedged in its sides, but now the rhino, in pain as well as anger, stormed on straight into the men. Its horn tossed a hunter into the air. Another man was dragged under its stamping hooves. The hunters wrestled with it, pressing their bone-barbed harpoons in to tear

its flesh. As the rhino weakened,
its great weight collapsed onto
the ground, shaking the valley floor.
Ja thrust a blade flake into its thick
neck for the fatal blow.

Jason stepped back from the rhino's
corpse and collapsed onto the ground.
His body was covered in blood, but
although he ached from bruising, he
had not been hurt. The women rushed
over to tend to the wounded hunters.
They tore off the leather from their
clothes to tie around the gaping
gashes on the hunters' bodies.

Once he had regained his breath, Jason walked over to the group of young girls. He wrapped his arms around his shaking, weeping sister in a comforting hug. He felt a strong hand on his shoulder. He turned around, and Ja was standing over him.

"Your bravery saved her," Ja grunted, before turning back to help carry the injured back to the cave.

Back at the cave, the women heated weeds and roots, and then crushed them to make a paste to cover the hunters' wounds. In one corner, two hunters lay severely injured. Over them stood a shaman wearing a bird headdress and a black, crow-feathered cloak. He had appeared at the cave shortly after the clan's return.

Propped against the cave wall, Jason watched the shaman in the flickering firelight. He listened to the shaman's mutterings and humming, as the

shaman became the bird spirit
to overcome death and heal and
revive the hunters. The shaman had
sacrificed an ox and now held its
still-beating heart above the hunters.
Then the shaman lifted each man's
head so that the man could drink
the ox's blood to replenish his own
great loss of blood.

Through the night, the shaman
muttered his magical spells, and
the older women tended the other
injured men.

Jason was awoken by the first rays of the low autumn sun reaching into the cave. As he looked around, he was heartened to see the hunter who had been tossed by the rhino's horn sitting up and being fed. Next to him, though, lay the lifeless body of the hunter who had been crushed. His wife and daughter were covering his body in red ochre powder, a type of red soil, as they wept. His son stood by gravely, aware of the responsibility he now had to take on.

Once the midday sun had reached its height, the bird-headed shaman reappeared. He led the procession of the clan out of the cave and along the ridge of the hill to where a grave had been dug that morning. Ja and five other hunters carried the dead hunter's reddened corpse wrapped in the ox's skin. They respectfully lowered the body into the hole.

Around the neck of the body was a necklace with five of the rhino's teeth. The son then laid his father's hunting tools alongside the body. Finally, with a grand gesture, the shaman lowered the rhino's horn engraved with horses, bison and an ibex into the grave. Silence fell.

What 'responsibility' was the hunter's son aware he would have to take on?

Are You a Hunter or a Gatherer?

Many behaviours people display today date back to our hunter-gatherer ancestors. Which behaviours have you inherited? Take this quiz to see whether you are a hunter or a gatherer.

1 You are on a road trip but are lost and do not know which way to go. What do you do?

a. Use a map to figure out how to get there.

b. Stop and ask for directions.

c. Go wherever the road takes you.

2 You go shopping to buy a new pair of shoes. What is your strategy?

a. You always buy the same shoes from the same shop — you head straight there and get it over with.

b. You look in several different shops and try on six pairs before making a decision.

c. You do not buy shoes; you make them!

3 Your younger brother borrows something without asking. How do you react?

a. You become angry and confront him.

b. You tell him politely to ask you first next time.

c. You are not interested in material possessions. He can keep it!

4 Your dad has misplaced his glasses.
Are you able to help him?

a. Nope. You know he was wearing them a second ago, but you do not have a clue where they are either.

b. Of course! You have a perfect memory of him leaving them on the table in the living room.

c. Maybe. You suggest he try reading through two glasses from the kitchen.

5 A friend calls you up to arrange to go to the cinema. How does it go?

a. You agree on a time and hang up. You have nothing else to say!

b. You launch into a conversation and end up on the phone for an hour.

c. You don't use phones; you communicate telepathically!

6 Which of these sports would you rather play?

a. Football

b. Horse riding

c. Hide-and-seek

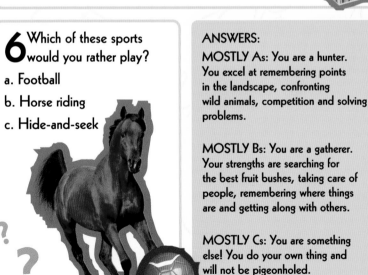

ANSWERS:

MOSTLY As: You are a hunter. You excel at remembering points in the landscape, confronting wild animals, competition and solving problems.

MOSTLY Bs: You are a gatherer. Your strengths are searching for the best fruit bushes, taking care of people, remembering where things are and getting along with others.

MOSTLY Cs: You are something else! You do your own thing and will not be pigeonholed.

Crime Scene Investigation:

Liguria

A body has been found in a cave in Liguria, Italy. No one knows who it is or how it got here. The police have sent a team of forensic specialists to gather clues.

1. Skull size and shape indicate that this is the body of a *Homo sapiens*.

2. Ornaments and personal possessions suggest that the person was wealthy.

3. Teeth provide clues about the person's age. This person was about 15 years old.

4. Shape of pelvis indicates that this skeleton is male.

5. Carefully arranged body suggests ceremonial burial.

6. Length of femur (leg bone) allows for the person's height to be calculated.

7. Location of burial provides clues about nearby historical events or settlements.

8. The body was found in a bed of red ochre. The meaning of this is uncertain.

CRIME SCENE - DO NOT CROSS - CRIME SCENE

73

Unexplained Symbols

Scientists have found repeating symbols in cave art around the world. The percentages of sites that contain each symbol are given below. It is not known what these symbols mean.

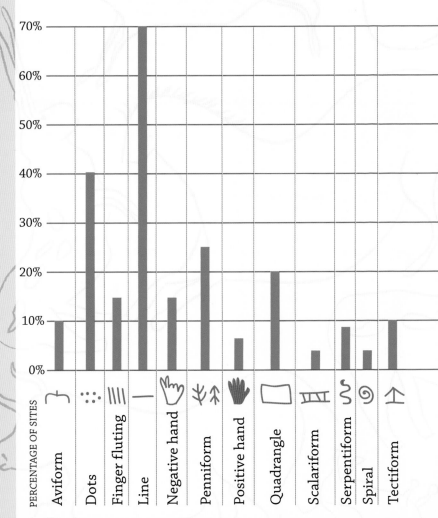

Painting in the Axial Gallery at
Lascaux showing typical symbols.

Quadrangle and lines

Aviform

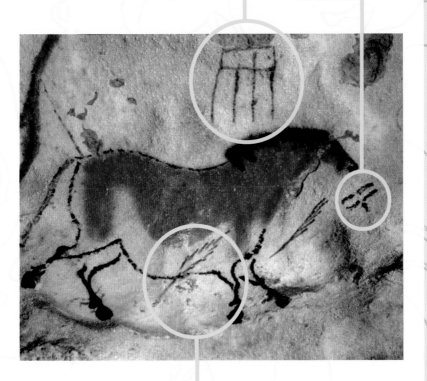

Penniform

CHAPTER FIVE
The Handprint

The winter had been a harsh one. At times, even the reindeer had not made much of an effort to escape the hunters. The snow had fallen thickly and covered the ground for some weeks. Staying warm had been the clan's greatest struggle. They had moved to a different cave with tunnels leading deeper into the rock. This gave them more warmth and protection. The clan persevered, and their greatest success was when the hunters killed a woolly mammoth. This fed the clan for a month.

Early one spring morning, Jason was woken by the chorus of singing birds. He lay awake listening to the others' breathing while they slept. His mind wandered to the days ahead – today his initiation would begin. Everything that he had been learning would be tested. "Do I know enough?" he wondered anxiously. "Will I succeed in finding a deer or even a stag? How many days will it take me?" He knew he could never face his father if he failed. He lay awake as the rest of the clan gradually stirred to life.

The women made a great fuss
over Jason during the first meal of
the day. He munched through thick
slabs of tender reindeer meat, chewy
plant roots and turnip-like tubers.
By the time he had finished, he felt
as if he was about to burst, but he did
not know when he would eat again.
The next meal he would have would
be one that he caught, prepared and
cooked all by himself. He would be
on his own.

   The whole clan gathered at the
entrance to the cave for his departure.
Jason was cloaked in a warm bison
skin, and over his shoulder, he slung
his leather pouch filled with tools:
antler bones to be used as hammers,
a borer to make holes, a burin for
carving wood or bone, an end-scraper
for removing fur and fats from meat,
and blade flakes for attaching to
the tips of his spear.

Jason filled a hollowed-out bone with some crushed red ochre and then blew the powder over his right hand, as he pressed it on the wall. The handprint marked the start of his initiation. Jasmine gave him a great big hug and then retreated to her mother's side. Picking up his spear, Jason stepped out into the crisp, cold morning air and took the path down into the valley. The clan returned to the warmth of the cave. Only Ja remained watching from the entrance until his son was out of sight.

Jason followed the familiar route down into the valley and across to the forest. The still-wintry trees looked skeletal, with bare branches reaching to grab the sky.

"Caw, caw." A crow's call resonated through the trees. Jason shivered – he did not like crows. Distracted, he stumbled over a tree root and stubbed his toe.

"Argh!" His yell disturbed a clamour of rooks, which flew up into the sky like a foreboding black cloud.

With dampened spirits, Jason headed deeper into the forest. He knew that this was likely to be the best place to find a deer or a stag. To begin with, the paths were familiar to him, but as the day progressed, he entered unknown territory. The monotony of walking made his mind drift to thinking about his clan and what they would be doing now. He pictured them eating around a warm fire, which made him feel hungry.

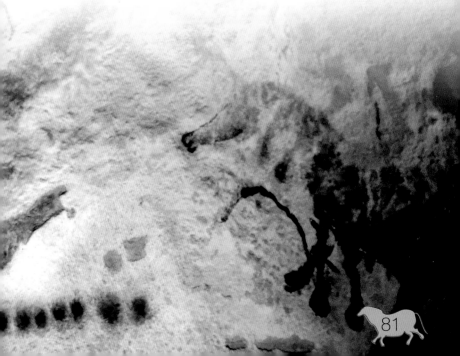

He could not get the thought of food out of his mind, no matter how hard he tried. He scanned the forest floor, but nothing moved. He took a blade flake from his pouch and scraped away some bark from the nearest tree.

He had chosen the slightly bulging point well, for underneath lay a fat beetle larva. It squirmed in shock at having suddenly been exposed to the cold air. Jason scooped it out with the blade and popped it into his mouth. "Juicy, but a bit chewy," he thought, "and with just a hint of wood flavour."

He found and ate a few more, but then this made him feel thirsty. He realised that he had no idea where the nearest stream or river was, and the sun was getting lower in the sky. He needed to abandon the hope of finding a stag and focus on surviving the night. He had to find a suitable location that would also provide some protection from the wind and rain.

A little way off, he spotted a glade of pine trees. Heading in that direction, he picked up long sticks and broke off branches as he walked. Jason chose a strong, thick tree and dropped his pouch full of tools next to it. He stood up, closed his eyes and sensed the wind direction on his face. Then he picked up the sticks and branches one by one and leaned them against the side of the chosen tree trunk out of the wind. Gradually, a tent shape formed. Nearby, a crow watched from its perch on a thick, moss-covered fallen log.

Jason's hands were cut and bruised, but he kept going. Using his blades, he broke off pine branches, which he used to cover the structure. The needles scraped and ripped his skin, but he persisted.

The sun started to go down, and all warmth was gone for the day. Jason had not noticed, however, because he was warmed by his work. After laying a final branch, he stepped back to admire his handiwork. "I'll be as cosy as a beetle larva snuggled in the bark," he thought.

It was tempting to rest inside his bivouac, but one more task needed to be accomplished – a fire to scare away the night predators. Gathering some short, dry twigs, he built them into the shape of a tiny teepee, with an open face directed into the wind. He placed some dry moss and sticks inside it. Bending low, he scraped a blade flake, striking the flint skilfully. A spark from the strike caught the moss on fire. The wind fanned the flames and within a few moments, Jason had a warming and glowing fire.

He sat back, suddenly hit by a wave of exhaustion from all of his efforts. He had finished just as the last of the sun's orange glow disappeared. Jason gazed up through the gap in the pine trees and saw the stars appearing in the increasing darkness. Sparkling right above his head were his favourite ones: when he linked them together in his mind, he saw a hunter in the sky.

A howl broke through the silence of the night. Jason nervously stoked the fire and then crawled inside his snug bivouac. Wrapping his bison-skin cloak around him, he lay down, and sleep quickly overwhelmed him.

Build a Cosy Bivouac

Jason makes himself a bivouac as shelter while he is out in the forest. If you ever find yourself stuck in the woods, here is how to make a bivouac of your own.

1. Wedge a forked branch in the ground and place a long, sturdy pole in the fork, with the other end in the ground. Check that it is long enough to sleep under, with about 60 cm (2 ft) to spare.

2. Create an A-frame for the door by resting sturdy diagonal poles opposite each other and meeting at the fork. If necessary, use twine or plant stems to tie the main frame together.

3. Lean short poles against the ridge, checking that you have room to lie down inside and to turn over in your sleep. Be sure that they do not protrude more than 4 cm (1½ in.) above the ridge pole.

4. If you have a sheet, drape it over the top and hold it down with rocks or sharp sticks. If not, cover the poles with a thick layer of leaves overlapped like roof tiles so that they do not let any rain through.

5. Hold the leaves down with a covering of thin brushwood. Pile dry grass or pine needles inside the shelter to prevent you from losing heat through the ground. Then slide in and block the entrance.

Light a Campfire

Another thing both you and Jason will need in the woods is a fire. This will help to scare off animals that might harm you, provide light, keep you warm and cook food. Here is how to make one.

YOU WILL NEED THESE ITEMS:

firewood

flint*

piece of iron pyrite (fool's gold)*

tinder (dead leaves or grass)

*You can use matches, if you do not have pyrite and flint.

1 Create a platform of sticks. Lay two thick logs parallel to each other on the edges of the platform.

2 Start building layers of sticks between the logs. Each layer should be at a right angle to the last. As the construction grows, you can place tinder in the central space.

3 You will need four, five or even six layers built on top of one another, depending on the thickness of the wood.

4 Use the flint to strike the piece of iron pyrite near the tinder. This should produce sparks to light the tinder.

You now have a fire!

Warning! Get an adult to help you.

Survival Kit

Compass
To figure out which direction you are going in.

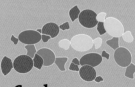

Torch
To find your way in the dark.

Whistle
To call for help, so rescuers can find you or to frighten animals away.

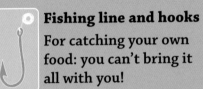

Candy
In an emergency, these provide a quick boost of energy.

Fishing line and hooks
For catching your own food: you can't bring it all with you!

When Jason set off for the forest, he brought a kit containing various tools made of flint and bone. If you go out into the woods, you will need a kit of your own that is nothing like Jason's. Here are a few of the things you will need.

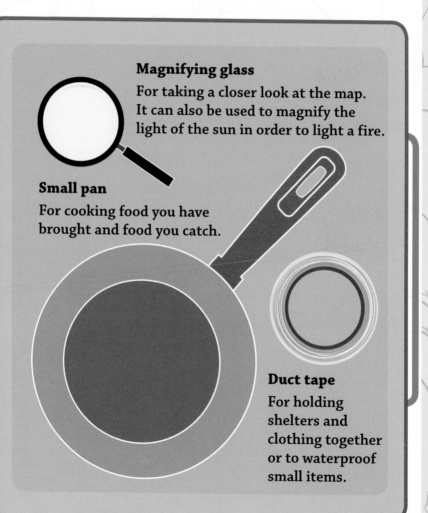

Magnifying glass

For taking a closer look at the map. It can also be used to magnify the light of the sun in order to light a fire.

Small pan

For cooking food you have brought and food you catch.

Duct tape

For holding shelters and clothing together or to waterproof small items.

CHAPTER SIX
The Black Stag

A cold, wet raindrop dripped from the roof of the bivouac, startling Jason awake. Outside, rain pelted down noisily. Every now and then, other drips came through the bivouac, but not many. He was proud to see that the structure and the canopy of the pine tree were protecting him well. Thinking quickly, he cupped his hands and reached out to collect some raindrops to drink. The water tasted refreshing and sweet, quenching his thirst.

The rainstorm dragged on and on. Jason lay awake restlessly. The cramped conditions made his legs ache, and he could not stand properly to stretch them. His frustration grew as he sat cooped up. "Would I be a fool to go out and try to hunt in the rain? If I did, how would I get dry afterwards? Where are these deer anyway?"

As Jason thought, he idly picked up his spear and started chipping away at the handle with his burin. As the morning passed, the face of a stag with its grand antlers formed on the handle.

Suddenly, Jason heard a rustling noise just outside the bivouac. He froze with his hand held mid-chip. The rustle moved closer, and Jason could sense the creature rubbing against the branches. Jason's heart pounded.

A small, brown mouse appeared and scampered over Jason's feet. Without moving a muscle, Jason watched the small creature scurry around, even allowing it to run up his leg. Then he remembered how hungry he was. After all, he needed food to survive. Here was a meal served within easy reach. Jason had to decide whether to let the mouse live and allow himself to starve, or to take the mouse's life to save his own. Jason's survival instincts won, and he knocked the mouse out with a single blow to its head. The rain continued to pour down.

It was early afternoon when the rain eased to a few occasional drips. Jason crawled out, desperate to stretch his legs. Everywhere, it was soggy and muddy. He could smell the sweet fragrance of the damp pine trees.

Knowing he did not have much time, he grabbed his leather pouch and spear and headed out. His moccasins were quickly soaked through from the damp forest floor, and this made his feet wet, too. Still he crept on, trying to be as quiet as possible so that he did not disturb any animals. He looked deep into the forest to find his target prey, but it was hopeless. Jason only came across a young wild boar rooting around for truffles. His stealthy ambush caught the boar unawares. It was an easy kill.

As yet another day drew to a close, Jason headed back to his glade. He made and lit a fire and cooked chopped chunks of boar meat. Although well fed, he lay back looking up at the night sky, feeling despondent. A shooting star whisked through the dark sky. Jason's spirits lifted, but just for a moment.

The sound of a howl made him shiver. It was closer than the previous night. With senses alert, Jason listened to the rustles of the small nocturnal animals around him. "More mice," he thought. Another howl and another in return echoed through the forest. "What made that noise – a wolf or some wild cats?" he worried.

Suddenly, a whoosh of silent wings flew over Jason's head, pounced on a scurrying creature and swooped away, gripping its victim in its talons.

Shaken by the owl's unexpected ambush, Jason stoked the fire until it was roaring. He did not want to be dinner for a wild creature. With a hand on the spear by his side, Jason sat, watching the shadows, desperately trying to keep his eyes open.

Jason jolted himself awake. Annoyed with himself for dozing, he gripped his spear firmly. Moonlight flooded the glade in a silvery glow. As he checked his surroundings, Jason caught sight of a silhouetted figure on the edge of the glade. The dark figure had a head shaped like a stag. Jason felt chills up his spine. "Was this a spirit or a stag?"

The figure stood proudly, directly watching Jason. Then it seemed to beckon him, before turning and heading into the moonlit forest. As if he were under a spell, Jason picked up his pouch and spear and followed. He did not know what made him go, but he knew he could not stop. The majestic creature strutted on. Jason dared not get too close. "What if the creature is luring me into a trap?" he wondered.

The figure led on and on, weaving through the forest. Jason had to duck under branches, leap over logs and squelch through muddy puddles. Once, Jason lost his footing and slipped in the mud. As he fell, his cloak and body were splattered with the wet mud, but the stag figure just stopped and waited at a distance until Jason caught his breath before continuing.

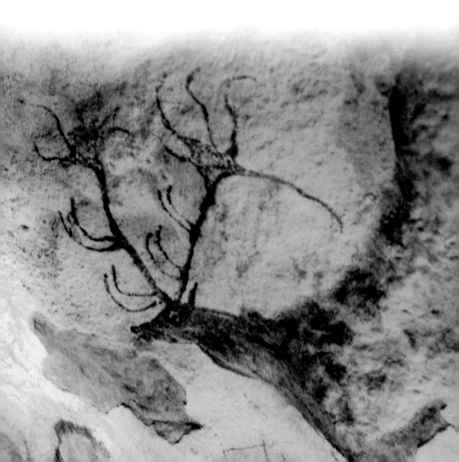

As dawn broke, Jason emerged from the forest beside a wide river. The dark figure had suddenly vanished. A movement in the water caught his eye. Swimming across the river towards him was a stag. Jason quickly ducked and, bending low, crawled behind a rocky boulder. There he waited for the stag to come ashore. As the river's edge became shallower, the stag with long, splendid antlers rose majestically out of the water.

Jason's heartbeat quickened as he sensed the stag moving closer. Its breath made white puffs in the cold air. Jason peeked around the boulder. He gasped. He had never seen a stag this close before. It stood tall and proud, holding its head high; its powerful body, supported by its four long, sleek legs, heaved from the exertion of the swim. Jason was impressed, but he had a task to achieve, and this was his moment. His one thought was to aim true. "Please let this be a quick, respectful death for the sake of this incredible creature," he muttered to himself, clutching his spear tightly.

Why did Jason's heartbeat quicken?

101

Slowly, Jason stood up from behind his boulder and took aim with his spear. For a split second, time stood still as the stag caught his scent and turned to face him. Their eyes met, but Jason had already released his spear. Soaring like an arrow, the spear fired straight, and the sharp-pointed blade struck directly into the stag's neck.

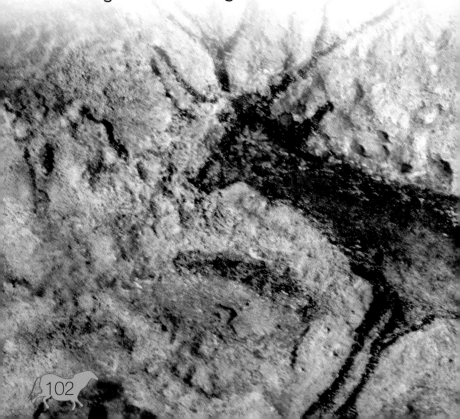

The stag fell, closed its eyes and exhaled its final breath.

Jason approached and cautiously reached out his hands to touch the still-warm body. The thick fur felt soft through his fingers. He sank to his knees, suddenly overwhelmed with exhaustion. He leaned his head on the body as if it were a pillow and closed his eyes.

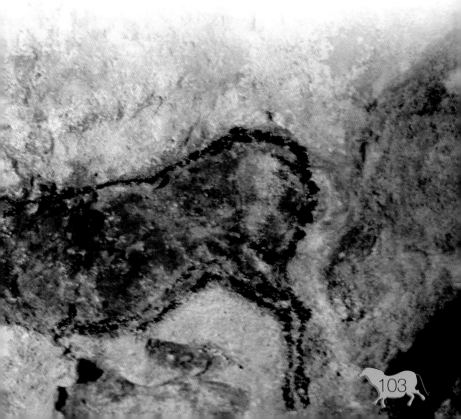

Spotter's Guide to the Animals of Lascaux

Palaeolithic wall paintings are filled with animals. Many of these animals are similar to modern animals, although the actual species are mostly extinct. Here are a few of the animals depicted.

Auroch

This was the ancestor of today's cattle, although it was a bit larger. It was eventually hunted into extinction. The last auroch was killed in 1627.

DATE Pleistocene (2.6 million to 11,700 years ago)
SIZE 3 m (10 ft) long
LOCATION Europe, Asia, North Africa

Horse

Horses have changed very little since prehistoric times. From about 10,000 to 500 years ago, they were extinct in North America but have existed continuously in the region of Lascaux for millions of years.

DATE Pliocene (5.3 to 2.6 million years ago) to present
SIZE 2.5 m (8¼ ft) tall
LOCATION Worldwide

*M*egaloceros

The *Megaloceros* was one of the largest deer ever known. It was about the size of a modern-day moose. Its antlers were used by the people of Lascaux to craft tools.

DATE Late Pliocene to late Pleistocene
SIZE 2.7 m (8¾ ft) long
LOCATION Europe, Asia

Woolly Mammoth

Mammoths were much like modern elephants in appearance – their DNA is almost identical to that of modern elephants – but their tusks were much longer and curved inwards.

DATE Pliocene to late Pleistocene
SIZE 5 m (16½ ft) tall
LOCATION North America, Europe, Asia, Africa

Woolly Rhinoceros

The woolly rhinoceros was about the size of a large white rhino today. It had a thick coat of long, shaggy hair, and a pair of horns that curved backwards.

DATE Pleistocene
SIZE 3.7 m (12¼ ft) long
LOCATION Europe, Asia

Book Review
by Maggie Ian, Books Editor

Title: *Stig of the Dump*

Author: Clive King

Publisher: Puffin

Clive King's *Stig of the Dump* is an enduring modern classic. King tells the imaginative and captivating story of a boy and his secret best friend – a caveman called Stig.

First published in 1963, *Stig of the Dump* introduces a boy named Barney, who tumbles down to the bottom of an old, disused chalk quarry and finds Stig living at the bottom. Stig comes up with a wealth of innovative ways for recycling all of the junk that people throw into the quarry into building his den.

He even adds some useful and surprisingly modern features, such as a chimney and some plumbing.

The friends embark on a range of exciting adventures, each more entertaining and enthralling than the last. King is wonderful at drawing the reader into the story and at making Stig and Barney's escapades come alive, all the while infusing their tale with both humour and warmth.

Together, you, Stig and Barney will come face-to-face with a leopard who has escaped from the zoo, catch some burglars breaking into Barney's grandparents' house and join a fox hunt (while protecting the fox). You will even travel back to prehistoric times with Stig to help his people erect one final standing stone before the sun comes up.

Delightful exploits aside, *Stig of the Dump* is, most importantly, a story about friendship and the carefree experience of childhood. Stig may be from the Stone Age, but his loyalty and spirit are timeless.

Imaginative yet believable, funny, adventurous and heart warming, it's a fantastic story for the young – and the young at heart.

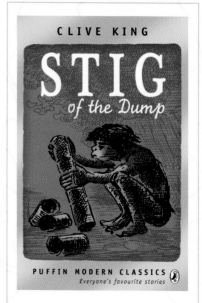

Stig is described as someone with a lot of shaggy hair and two bright black eyes. He wears a rabbit skin and speaks in grunts.

CHAPTER SEVEN
The Sorcerer

The sound of an excited flock of water birds soaring overhead woke Jason. As he became aware of his surroundings, he noticed the water rippling with splashes. Silvery pink fish were leaping and swimming against the water current. "Salmon!" he gasped.

Quickly, he pulled out his spear from the neck of the stag. He removed the blade and strapped a sharp new one in its place. Moving down to the water's edge, he took off his mud-caked shoes and waded into the cool river. He could feel the salmon brushing against his legs in their hurry to swim upstream to their spawning grounds.

With the calm of an experienced hunter, Jason steadied his gaze and sensed the movement of the fish. Then he plunged his spear into the water. The blade hit its mark. He lifted out a wriggling salmon, which he pulled off the blade and tossed over to the riverbank. Again, he deftly speared another. Back on the riverbank, Jason made a fire. He chopped up the fish and then cooked each piece held on the end of a stick in the flames. He ate hungrily.

Full after his feast, Jason walked back to the water's edge and scooped up the refreshing water. He drank and washed. Strengthened once more, he could now face his final task: removing the head of the dead stag to carry home.

He diligently set to work – something he had done many times on other beasts during training. This was somehow different. His blade struck with care and respect for the spirit of the dead animal.

The task completed, he strapped the head to his back with strips of leather and followed the river upstream towards home. The rocky cliffs towering above him soon became the landmarks he knew well. His steps quickened, and as he rounded a river bend, the valley opened up before him.

Jasmine, who had been sitting patiently at the entrance of the cave

awaiting her brother's return, was
the first to see him. She called to the
others and then ran down the path
to greet him.

As Jason entered the cave with the
stag's head, he caught Ja's eyes looking
at him, and saw
that his gaze was
one of proud
approval. Jason
had left as
a boy, but was
now welcomed
back as a man.

Why did Jason feel his
final task was somehow
different this time?

As dusk fell, the clan made its way to the cave at Lascaux. Torches lit their route through the winding cavernous passageways to the most sacred area. There a shaman wearing a stag headdress was humming and swaying over a fire. Jason was reminded of the stag-headed dark figure that he had followed.

The clan formed a circle around the fire and joined in the hum. As the smoke from the fire rose and swirled around, the shaman entered into a trance. Jason stepped forwards and presented the head of his stag to him. With cries appealing to the spirit of the stag, the shaman lifted the head high and chanted mutterings, weaving spells of future hunting success for Jason.

In the flickering torchlight, Jason added some cave water to some red ochre. Then he dipped his fingers into

the red mixture and drew an outline
of a stag onto the wall. As he did
so, he remembered the stag standing
majestically on the riverbank.
The spirit of his stag would live on in
this painting, long after Jason's time.

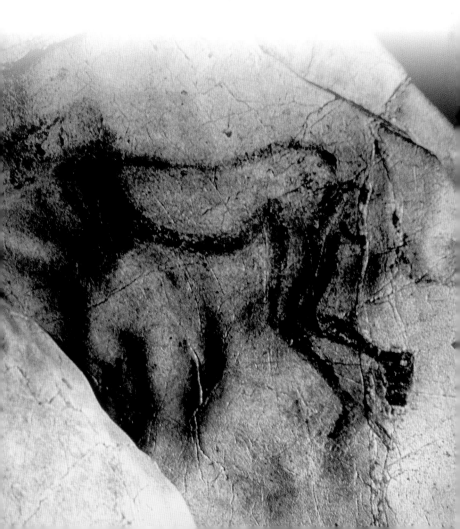

La Nouvelle

22 February, 1947

REVEALED: FIRST PHOTOGRAPHS OF ANCIENT FRENCH CAVE PAINTINGS

By Pierre LaRocque

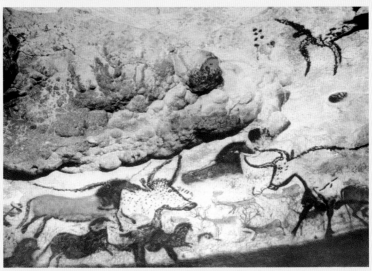

Montignac, France – Ralph Morse has become the first professional photographer to capture the Lascaux cave paintings.

The caves of Lascaux were discovered several years ago, but the troubles suffered by France during World War II had kept their existence secret until a short time ago.

"I was working in the Paris bureau after the War. We received a message from New York about this cave in the south of France that people were talking about. After some investigation, we learned that the caves had been discovered during the War, but no one had ever photographed them," Morse said.

M. Parvaud, Léon Larval, Marcel Ravidat and Jacques Marsal in Montignac, France.

The caves were discovered on 12 September, 1940, by Jacques Marsal, aged 14; Marcel Ravidat, aged 17; Georges Agniel, aged 15; and Simon Coencas, aged 13.

"It was really Robot, my dog, who discovered them," said Ravidat soon after the discovery. "We were hunting rabbits on a ridge, and Robot chased one down into a hole, so we decided to investigate."

The boys returned a few days later. Marcel was the first one in, and he described what he saw: "We came into an enormous room and raised our lanterns up. Then we saw all these big, colourful animal figures – there was a bull that was about 4.5 metres long. Our joy was indescribable."

The boys were the first visitors to the Great Hall of the Bulls in 17,000 years. Prehistorian Henri Breuil confirmed the authenticity of the paintings.

The boys' excitement has now been echoed seven years later, when Morse crawled into the muddy cave to take his pictures.

Of his visit, he said, "We couldn't believe what we saw. The paintings looked brand new and were absolutely enormous," Morse said.

Morse's photographs will appear in the 24 February, 1947 issue of *Life* magazine.

Rock Art from Around the World

Rock art was not just in France – it was all over the world! Here is some rock art from cultures across the globe.

Oenpelli, Arnhem Land, Australia
Date uncertain

Plant and mineral pigments were used in ancient Aboriginal rock art, such as this painting of a turtle.

Inanke Cave, Zimbabwe
10,000–3,000BCE

This painting by the San people of southern Africa depicts antelope, which are believed to provide a link with the spirit world.

Fossum, Sweden
1,700–500BCE

These rock carvings show men, deer and boats. The boats may symbolise the sea or the sun's daily journey.

Bhimbetka, India
c.10,000BCE–c.500CE

This painting on the inner wall was made using vegetable pigments and shows a procession of warriors on horses.

Make Cave Art: Creating Colours

You can make your own cave art just like the paintings at Lascaux. Here is how to do it.

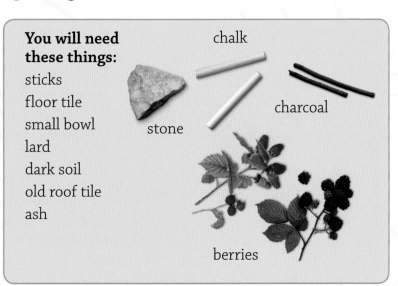

You will need these things:

sticks
floor tile
small bowl
lard
dark soil
old roof tile
ash

chalk

charcoal

stone

berries

stick

berries

1 Crush the berries. Using a stick, mix them with a little water to make a smooth, red paste.

2 Mix the dark soil with a spoonful of lard. Add more soil to make the 'paint' darker and less greasy, or more lard if the paint is too dry.

lard

dark soil

stone

chalk

roof tile

3 Using the roof tile as a slab, crush the chalk with a stone, grinding it to a powder. Mix this powder with water to make a white paste.

4 Mix the ash with a little water to make a grey paste, adding more water or ash to get the right texture.

ash

Make Cave Art: Get Painting!

charcoal

5 With charcoal or a burned stick, draw a bison's body on your floor tile. Use simple lines and straight-sided shapes.

6 Draw a triangle with stick horns for the head, and add a stick man in front of the animal, running away.

berry and soil paste

7 With your fingers, fill in the bison with the brown paint made by mixing the berry and soil pastes together. Use plenty of paste. It darkens as it dries.

8 Mix the chalk and ash pastes. Smudge this onto parts of the face and back to highlight these areas.

chalk and ash paste

9 Use a charcoal stick to darken the hooves and the end of the tail.

Your finished piece

Prehistoric Quiz

See if you can remember the answers to these questions about what you have read.

1. Approximately how long ago did the first modern humans appear?

2. Why does the clan expect Jason to become a great hunter?

3. What 'sign' does Jason see as he returns with the horse meat?

4. Which early human species lived alongside *Homo sapiens*?

5. Which tool was used by prehistoric man to carve delicate pictures?

6. Who is the half-man, half-unicorn figure?

7. Which star cluster can be found in the constellation Taurus?

8. How does Jason give the hunters' position away to the bison?

9. Why is it important for the women to pick every single nut and fruit?

10. What can the length of a skeleton's leg bone tell us about its owner?

11. What symbol in the cave marks the start of Jason's initiation?

12. What does Jason see in the sky on the first night of his initiation?

13. Which animal was the ancestor of today's cattle?

14. What is Jason's final task?

15. What was the name of the dog who discovered Lascaux?

Answers on page 125.

Glossary

Crescendo
Gradual increase in loudness.

Despondent
In low spirits.

Diligently
Carefully.

Glade
Open, grassy area in a forest.

Initiation
Introduction to a special group.

Maim
To cause serious injury or disfigure someone.

Mayhem
Disorder.

Moccasin
Type of soft shoe made of leather.

Pigment
Natural, dry, colour powder that is mixed with water or oil to make paint.

Prehistoric
Time before writing existed.

Shaman
Person who uses magic to link the natural and supernatural worlds.

Silhouette
The dark outline of something.

Stampede
Sudden rush of a group of frightened animals.

Summon
To call for someone.

Talons
Bird's claws.

Trance
State of unconsciousness.

Tuber
Type of vegetable that comes from the roots of a plant.

Index

Answers to the Prehistoric Quiz:

1. 200,000 years ago; **2.** Because his father Ja is a great hunter; **3.** A crow; **4.** *Homo neanderthalensis*; **5.** Burin; **6.** The shaman; **7.** The Pleiades; **8.** He yells as he slips on a pile of dung; **9.** To help the clan through the forthcoming winter; **10.** The owner's height; **11.** His handprint; **12.** The hunter star formation; **13.** The auroch; **14.** Removing the head of the stag and taking it home; **15.** Robot.

Guide for Parents

DK Reads is a three-level interactive reading adventure series for children, developing the habit of reading widely for both pleasure and information. These chapter books have an exciting main narrative interspersed with a range of reading genres to suit your child's reading ability, as required by the National Curriculum. Each book is designed to develop your child's reading skills, fluency, grammar awareness, and comprehension in order to build confidence and engagement when reading.

Ready for a *Reading Alone* book

YOUR CHILD SHOULD

- be able to read independently and silently for extended periods of time.
- read aloud flexibly and fluently, in expressive phrases with the listener in mind.
- respond to what they are reading with an enquiring mind.

A VALUABLE AND SHARED READING EXPERIENCE

Supporting children when they are reading proficiently can encourage them to value reading and to view reading as an interesting, purposeful and enjoyable pastime. So here are a few tips on how to use this book with your child.

TIP 1 Reading aloud as a learning opportunity:

- if your child has already read some of the book, ask him/her to explain the earlier part briefly.
- encourage your child to read slightly slower than his/her normal silent reading speed so that the words are clear and the listener has time to absorb the information, too.

Reading aloud provides your child with practice in expressive reading and performing to a listener, as well as a chance to share his/her responses to the storyline and the information.

TIP 2 Praise, share and chat:

- encourage your child to recall specific details after each chapter.

- provide opportunities for your child to pick out interesting words and discuss what they mean.

- discuss how the author captures the reader's interest, or how effective the non-fiction layouts are.

- ask the questions provided on some pages and in the quiz. These help to develop comprehension skills and awareness of the language used.

- ask if there's anything that your child would like to discover more about.

Further information can be researched in the index of other non-fiction books or on the Internet.

A FEW ADDITIONAL TIPS

- Continue to read to your child regularly to demonstrate fluency, phrasing and expression; to find out or check information; and for sharing enjoyment.

- Encourage your child to read a range of different genres, such as newspapers, poems, review articles and instructions.

- Provide opportunities for your child to read to a variety of eager listeners, such as a sibling or a grandparent.

Series consultant **Shirley Bickler** is a longtime advocate of carefully crafted, enthralling texts for young readers. Her LIFT initiative for infant teaching was the model for the National Literacy Strategy Literacy Hour, and she is co-author of *Book Bands for Guided Reading* published by Reading Recovery based at the Institute of Education.

Have you read these other great books from DK?

READING ALONE

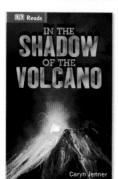

Dramatic modern-day adventure as Mount Vesuvius re-awakens.

Life-or-death futuristic space adventure to find a new home planet.

Pulse-racing action adventure chasing twisters in Tornado Alley.

Time-travelling adventure caught up in the intrigue in ancient Rome.

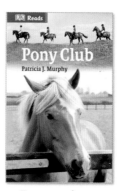

Emma adores horses. Will her wish come true at a riding camp?

Lucy follows her dream to train as a professional dancer.